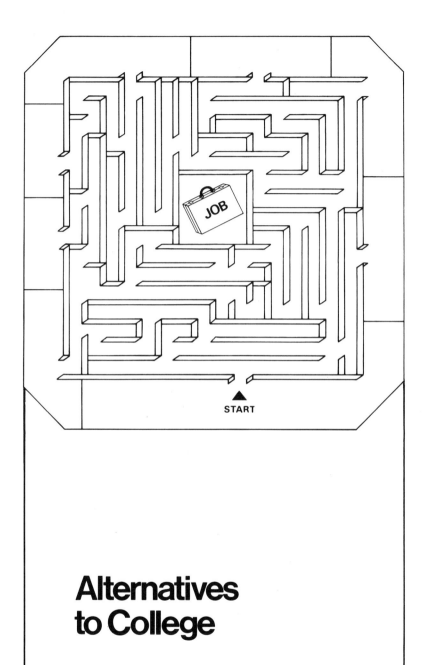

JOB

START

Alternatives
to College

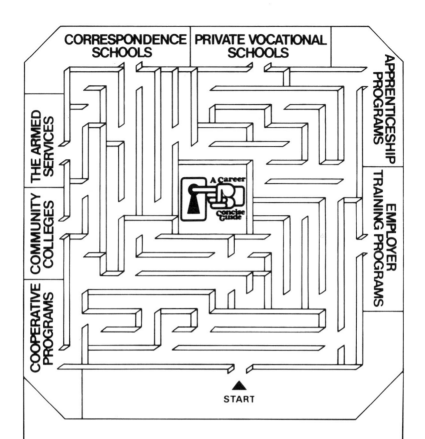

CORRESPONDENCE SCHOOLS

PRIVATE VOCATIONAL SCHOOLS

APPRENTICESHIP PROGRAMS

THE ARMED SERVICES

EMPLOYER TRAINING PROGRAMS

COMMUNITY COLLEGES

COOPERATIVE PROGRAMS

A Career Concise Guide

START

ALTERNATIVES TO COLLEGE
by Linda Atkinson

FRANKLIN WATTS | NEW YORK | LONDON | 1978

Library of Congress Cataloging in Publication Data

Atkinson, Linda.
    Alternatives to college.

    (A Career concise guide)
    Includes index.
    SUMMARY: Discusses programs of post-high
school education and training other than college,
including vocational schools, correspondence
schools, and employer training programs.
    1. Career education. 2. Vocational guidance.
3. Education, Higher. [1. Vocational guidance. 2.
Education, Higher] I. Title.
LC1037.A87   373.2'46   78–5957
ISBN 0–531–01495–9

Contents

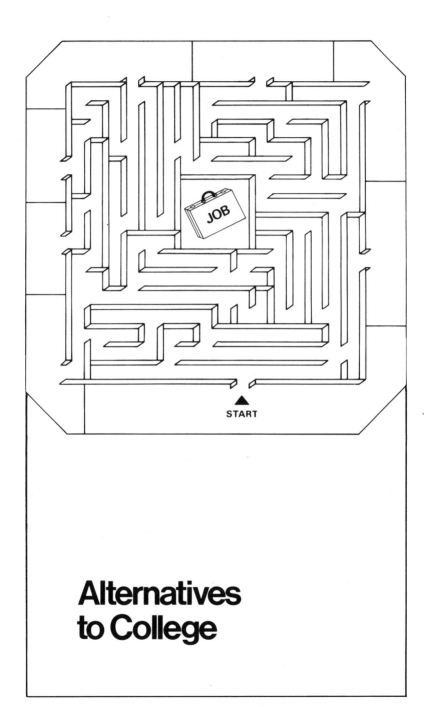

START

Alternatives
to College

The majority of students in college today are not happy there. They don't like to study. They don't like their classes or their instructors. They don't like anything about it.

Why are they there—at a cost of thousands of dollars a year? Many of them say they didn't know what else to do when they graduated from high school. Others say they went because all their friends were going, or because their parents expected it of them. But most of them are there because they think that without a college degree they will not be able to get a good job. And they think that with one a good job is just about guaranteed. They are wrong on both counts.

First: There are plenty of good jobs—high in interest and salary—that do not require a college education. The range is very wide: from medical assistants to plumbers, locomotive engineers to marine divers, computer programmers to hotel managers. There are crafts one can learn and trades by the score. The salaries in some of the trades are higher than the average salaries earned by college graduates. In fact, most of the people (58 percent) who earned $15,000 or more in 1972 were not college graduates. And according to the Department of Labor, in less than five years, 80 percent of all the new jobs in the United States will require not a college degree but vocational or technical training. Other sources say this is already true today.

Even in fields in which a college education is considered a basic requirement, people without degrees, but with real talent and drive, can make it. Carl Bernstein, one of the stars of 1970s journalism, is a college dropout. (Bernstein's colleague Bob Woodward has a B.A. from an Ivy League school.) Harry Truman never went to college at all.

Second: A college degree is not a ticket to a good job. Graduates of four-year liberal arts institutions have not been trained in any occupation and they have no specific "marketable" skills. They aim for positions, usually on the managerial level, in fields related to what they studied in college. Most of them don't find them. In the early 1970s, most college graduates (three quarters of the social science majors and two thirds of the humanities majors) could not find jobs that were related to their major fields. Instead, they became salespeople, hospital attendants, secretaries, bookkeepers, and typists, because those were the jobs that were available. (Most of the men wound up in sales, most of the women in clerical positions.)

This is not to say that going to a four-year liberal arts college is, in itself, a waste of time. College is what it has always been—a place to study under the inspection and guidance of scholars, a place to meet people and to learn. If that is what you want, college is not a waste of time for you. But if you are thinking about college because you believe that a college degree leads to a good job—or is necessary in order to get one—think again. Or better still, think fresh, new ideas. Look at some of the alternatives to college described in the following chapters. One of them may be right in line with what you really want to do.

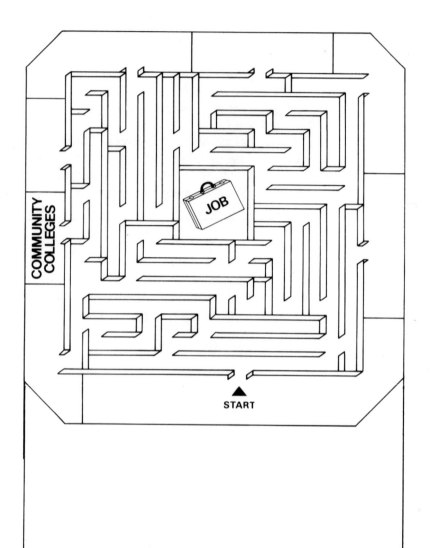

COMMUNITY
COLLEGES

JOB

START

Community
Colleges

WHAT THEY ARE,
WHAT THEY OFFER

Community colleges are two-year colleges that offer two kinds of programs. One is "academic" and consists of courses just like those given to freshmen and sophomores at four-year liberal arts colleges. The other program is "vocational." It trains students for jobs.

Students who complete an academic program are qualified to go on to a four-year college. Students who complete a vocational program are qualified for immediate employment.

Community colleges are found in almost every county in every state in the United States. Some are small, with enrollments of fewer than 1,000 students each year. Others are giant complexes, with sprawling campuses and enrollments of 40,000 students yearly. Some are residential and provide dormitories for their students, who come from all over the country. Others are strictly local. Their students live nearby and commute to the campus for their classes. These schools usually allow only local residents to enroll. If you come from another county or state, you may need special permission to attend, or you may have to pay a special fee.

Large or small, residential or commuter, almost all community colleges have a full campus life, with social events, clubs, student government, student newspapers, films, dances, and athletics. Vocational and academic students mix and mingle in extracurricular activities and take some of their classes together. The result is lively—and instructive—for both.

What kinds of jobs can you learn to do in a community college? The range is enormous. There are training programs for almost all the jobs in the "middle manpower" category—jobs that require up to but not more than two years of training after high school. Such jobs are found in business, industry, health, education, child care, public service, technology, and the trades. Here is a list of some major occupational areas and some of the programs community colleges offer in each.

[5]

Community colleges can prepare students for jobs in administration and management. Here, a Public Affairs Assistant studies micronegatives of photographs at the Environmental Protection Agency.

OCCUPATIONAL AREA	PROGRAMS COMMONLY OFFERED BY COMMUNITY COLLEGES
Business	Accounting
	Administration and Management
	Data Processing
	Sales and Retailing
	Secretarial Science
Engineering	Aero and Aerospace Technology
	Air Conditioning Technology
	Architectural Technology
	Chemical Technology
	Electrical and Electronic Technology
	Engineering Technology
	Industrial Technology
	Mechanical Technology
	Metallurgical Technology
Trades and Industry	Agriculture
	Aviation
	Clothing Technology
	Construction
	Dental Assisting
	Dental Hygiene
	Dental Technology
	Drafting
	Electricity and Electronics
	Food and Hotel Technology
	Forestry
	Home Economics
	Metal and Machine
	Nursing
	Physical Education and Recreation
	Police Science
	Printing

No community college provides training for all the jobs in all these areas. Instead, each school plans its own programs to meet the needs of its own community. Each tries to offer job training in fields where local jobs exist. In large cities, where there are an almost unlimited number of different kinds of jobs available, a community college may offer dozens of different programs. The New York City Community College in Brooklyn—only one of several community colleges that are part of the City University of New York—offers training in twenty-nine different occupations. In schools that serve smaller areas, fewer programs are offered, but some of those programs are unique. They are offered because they meet the needs of the specific job market in the area. In Montana, for example, the Flathead Valley Community College offers a training program in Timber Falling. Students learn how to fell trees and scale timber, as well as how to manage and operate a timber business. In California, the Santa Barbara Community College offers a program in Marine Diving Technology. Students are trained for jobs with the companies that prospect for oil off the California coast. A community college in Chicago has a Motor Transportation Program that trains students for supervisory and managerial positions in Chicago's booming trucking industry.

HOW LONG ARE THE PROGRAMS?

Community colleges follow the standard college calendar. The year is divided into two full semesters, September through January, and February through June. Students may attend either the day or the evening session. Sometimes "mini-semesters," which offer special projects and condensed courses, are held during the winter recess. Summer sessions, too, are usually available.

Most programs take two years of full-time day study to complete. If you enroll in the evening session, it will take longer. General studies courses—which are not related to the job in question—are a required part of the curriculum. When you complete the requirements of the two-year program, you receive an associate's degree in the field you studied.

"Accelerated Admissions Programs" are available at some schools. High school seniors, with the approval of their principal, are permitted to study at the college during what would normally be their last year of high school. At the end of the year, they receive their high school diplomas. If you know what you want to do, and are in a hurry to get started, an accelerated program may be for you.

This is the schedule of a student in the Architectural Technology Program offered by New York City Community College in Brooklyn. It is a two-year program leading to the degree Associate of Arts in Architectural Technology.

FIRST SEMESTER
Architectural Drawing I
Architectural Graphics I
History of Architectural Technology
Materials in Architecture
Fundamentals of Mathematics
English Composition I

SECOND SEMESTER
Architectural Drawing II
Architectural Graphics II
Methods of Construction in Architecture
Site Planning
Introduction to Mathematical Analysis
Elective (the course of your choice
    from the liberal arts curriculum)

THIRD SEMESTER
Architectural Drawing III
Design Appreciation and Analysis
Architectural Office Practice and Specifications
Architectural Environmental System
Physics I
Elective

FOURTH SEMESTER
Architectural Drawing IV
Architectural Space Analysis
Architectural Project Management
Principles of Stability in Structures
Elective

Not everyone who completes a vocational training program in a community college lands a good job—or even a job in the field for which they were trained. But the faculty and staff are well aware that getting a job is the important "last step" for the students who go through their programs. Help is offered all along the way. You will be told before you enroll about the specific jobs for which the program qualifies you. Most community colleges will also tell you the number of such jobs that exist—and how many are expected to exist in the future. They will give you the names of professional and other associations in the field that you may contact for further information. And when you finish the program, you may use the school's own placement service, which helps graduates find "first jobs." Most community colleges do an excellent job of placing their graduates. In one recent year, 85 percent of the graduates of the five community colleges of the City University of New York found jobs in their fields soon after completing their training. That is a record all prospective students should find encouraging.

HOW MUCH DOES IT COST?

Community colleges are public, tax-supported institutions. Most of them are almost or entirely tuition-free for local residents. Tuition at private "junior" colleges that offer the same kinds of programs average $1,000 a year.

Many two-year colleges offer programs in Food and Hotel Technology. These reservationists have their hands full confirming requests for rooms at a large hotel in San Francisco.

Scholarships and loans are available at the schools that charge tuition. And the federal government has many programs to help students at all community and junior colleges. Among them are Basic Educational Opportunity Grants, Supplemental Educational Opportunity Grants, and National Defense Student Loans. For more information about federal programs, contact the Financial Aid Office of the community or junior college nearest you, or write to Student Aid, U.S. Office of Education, Washington, D.C. 20202.

HOW TO APPLY

Telephone the Admissions Office of your local community college to find out about the programs it offers and the enrollment procedure. The number should be listed in your local telephone directory. If you do not know the name of the community college nearest you, write to the Director of Education, State Department of Education, in your state capital.

Most community colleges have an "open door" policy. They admit everyone who can make good use of their programs. In most cases, all you need is a high school diploma or the equivalent. Private junior colleges determine their own entrance requirements, but they are not usually very difficult to meet.

In both public community and private junior colleges, the Director of Admissions may want to interview you, and he or she may ask that your high school records be forwarded to the Admissions Office. Some schools ask that you be tested by the American College Testing Program. The results are used, not to determine whether or not you can enroll, but as sources of information for the guidance counselors who will help you plan your program.

For more information about community and junior colleges throughout the United States, write to the American Association of Community and Junior Colleges, One Dupont Circle N.W., Suite 410, Washington, D.C. 20036. And ask the reference librarian in your local library for the Association's *Directory of Community and Junior Colleges.*

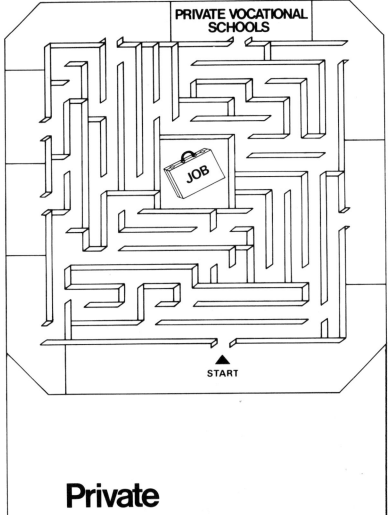

Private
Vocational
Schools

WHAT THEY ARE,
WHAT THEY OFFER

Private vocational schools are profit-making institutions that teach the specific skills needed to perform specific jobs. They do not offer courses in anything that is not directly related to the job or in things that employers do not consider important. The programs are as compact as possible, and students are encouraged to complete them as quickly as possible.

There are over 7,000 private vocational schools in the United States today. Almost all of them are small, with enrollments of about 300 students a year. The atmosphere is personal, uncomplicated, and friendly.

Usually these schools do not have campuses or buildings of their own. Most of them rent space in an area that is easy to reach by public transportation. They consist of a floor or two of classrooms, equipment, offices, and perhaps a lounge or a cafeteria. There are no extracurricular activities. These schools have only one aim: to turn out competent, employable people as quickly as possible. Most of them do it very well.

Training programs in over 200 different occupations are now available. Here is a list of some of the more popular ones—along with a few, like the program in baseball umpiring, that are truly unusual and are not offered by any other kind of school.

Accountant
Air Conditioning Repair and Maintenance
Announcer and Broadcaster: Radio and TV
Automotive Mechanic
Baker
Bartender
Baseball Umpire
Bookkeeper
Carpenter
Carpet Layer
Court Reporter

In our increasingly technological world, data processors and computer operators are becoming more and more important in most businesses and government agencies.

Data Processor
Dietician
Dog Groomer and Trainer
Draftsperson
Dressmaker
Electrolysist
Electronic Technician and Technologist
Embalmer
Fashion Designer
Floral Designer
Hairdresser and Cosmetologist
Hotel and Motel Manager
Interior Decorator and Designer
Jewelry Designer
Laboratory Technician and Technologist
Locksmith
Medical and Dental Assistant
Model
Piano Tuner and Repairer
Plumber
Printer
Restaurant Manager
Saddlemaker
Watchmaker

All private vocational schools "specialize": that is, they offer programs in only one vocational area, like electronics, or carpentry, or drafting. But within that area you can choose from occupations on different levels of difficulty. The schools try to present their material in "modules," or units, so that even after you have begun to study you can transfer from one program to another with very little loss of time. For example, you might enroll in a technical school to learn radio and TV repair, and then transfer to the more complicated program in electronic technology, which would prepare you to work on other kinds of electronic equipment, like computers, stereos, and processing machines. Or you might begin in the electronics program and transfer to the repair program.

[16]

The instruction is generally excellent. It has to be. The school's reputation depends on its ability to teach its students well—to turn out graduates employers will be happy to hire. It isn't a question of "getting you through the course," but of getting you to master the skills you need to do the job.

Classes are small. If you need extra practice or coaching, your teachers will see that you get it. They want you to succeed—that is their job. In fact, they are held accountable if their students do badly. If you do not understand the material, your teacher will break it down for you. If you need to go over it again, you may. Individual attention—and plenty of it—is the rule.

Many schools, especially those that train technicians and technologists, offer remedial or "makeup" courses for the student whose background has gaps in important areas. A drafting student, for example, may not have had enough math in high school—or may not have learned it well enough —to get on with the drafting courses. Technical schools are familiar with this kind of problem and are usually willing to work with the student for as long as it takes to bring him or her up to par.

Every vocational school has a placement service to help its graduates find jobs. In many schools, the placement service is "lifetime." You may ask for its help whenever you are looking for a job—even years after you have graduated. In the best schools, the placement service is excellent and helps to place 90 percent of the graduates. Some schools are so well known and respected that employers ask them for recommendations when they have positions to fill. A good vocational school is as good a referral center as it is a training center.

Does it ever make sense to choose a private vocational school when training for the same occupation is available free at a local community college? Some students think so. They prefer vocational schools because the programs are usually shorter, the classes more conveniently scheduled, and the placement services widely recognized. Private schools are smaller. Their programs can be (and usually are)

[17]

quickly changed to meet changes in the job market. The instructors, for the most part, are people who have earned their credentials in the working world. They may not have the academic degrees that members of the faculty in a community college have, but they often have more solid on-the-job experience. And these schools tend to be more student-centered than community colleges. The focus of everyone is on how well the student is learning.

If you want or need this kind of program, a private vocational school may be the right choice for you. But you must be careful. All these schools are run for profit, and though the great majority provide an excellent service for the fees they charge, some are badly run. A few are actually frauds. You must investigate before you enroll. If possible, visit the school, talk to the students, and look into the classrooms. Most schools will encourage you to do this. Ask at the Admissions Office for a copy of the school's "Annual Employment Summary," a fact sheet that lists the number of graduates in each program and the percentage who found jobs in their fields. All legitimate schools keep these records, and they will show them to you willingly. Finally, make sure the school you are considering is "accredited." That means it has been investigated and found to meet certain standards. If it is, find out the name of the accrediting agency. Call the Better Business Bureau or the Chamber of Commerce to see if any complaints have been made against the agency or the school. You can't go wrong if the school is accredited by the National Association of Trade and Technical Schools. It is recognized by the U.S. Office of Education. Schools that meet its standards are definitely up to par.

**Bookkeeping is only
one of many specialized
skills always needed
in the business world.**

HOW LONG ARE THE PROGRAMS?

Most programs can be completed in one year or less of full-time study (six hours a day, five days a week). A few, in complicated fields like engineering technology, may take as long as three years. Generally, however, students progress at their own rate. If you are a hard worker and can study full-time, you may be able to complete a two-year program in less than two years. If you are slow, or cannot attend full-time, the program may take you longer.

Private vocational schools operate year-round, spring, summer, fall, and winter, with a one-week winter recess and a one-week recess in July. New classes begin every month—in some schools every other week—throughout the year. You can enter a training program at almost any time.

Graduation occurs whenever you finish the courses. There is no formal ceremony and usually no formal degree. Instead, you will be given a certificate indicating that you have completed a specific course of study. More important, if things go as they should, you will soon have a good job.

HOW MUCH DOES IT COST?

Tuition at most private vocational schools ranges from $800 to $2,000 a year for students taking a full program. The cost depends upon the type of school, its location, the program, and the equipment used.

These schools do not offer scholarships, but many students work part-time, and most schools help them to find suitable jobs.

Most court reporters today use stenotypewriters to record court transcripts, a skill taught at many vocational schools.

The federal government has many programs to help young people who wish to study in a private vocational school. For information, write to Student Aid, U.S. Office of Education, Washington, D.C. 20202.

HOW TO APPLY

Every school determines its own entrance requirements, and most are quite selective about whom they will accept as students. If the school feels that you are not likely to do well in the program or on the job, it will not accept you— even though you are willing to pay the tuition. Some schools ask prospective students to take an aptitude test. But the decision is usually based primarily on your high school record, both academic and personal. Students who have done poorly in their classes, who have a spotty and irregular history in attendance, or who for other reasons have been considered "unmanageable" may be considered poor risks and refused admittance. Recommendations from your high school principal, teachers, or guidance counselor are often required.

For the names of schools and descriptions of the programs they offer, check the reference section of your local library for the *Directory of Accredited Private Trade and Technical Schools,* published by the National Association of Trade and Technical Schools. Or write to the Association, 2021 L Street N.W., Washington, D.C. 20009. Check your library for *Lovejoy's Career and Vocational School Guide,* by Clarence E. Lovejoy, and *Getting Skilled,* by John Coyne and Tom Hebert. Both should be available in the reference section. They contain a great deal of information, tips, and advice—and listings of almost every private vocational school in the country. You can also look in the Yellow Pages of your telephone directory (under "Schools") for listings of schools in your area.

When you find schools that offer programs in which you are interested, write to them. Ask for a catalog and information on how to apply. Be sure to investigate thoroughly before you make a decision.

[22]

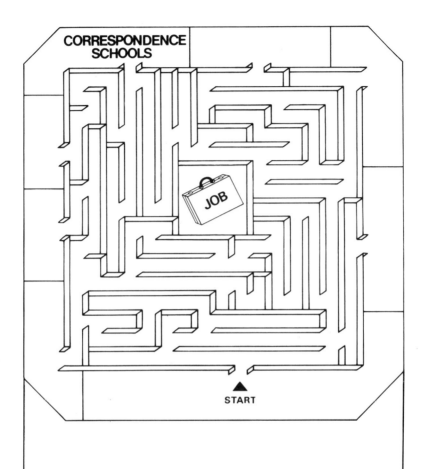
CORRESPONDENCE
SCHOOLS

JOB

START

Correspondence
Schools

WHAT THEY ARE,
WHAT THEY OFFER

Correspondence schools offer courses that have been specially designed to be completed at home. You receive everything you need through the mail: textbooks, study guides, assignments, tests, notes, and instructions prepared by a member of the teaching staff; tapes, records, and equipment when called for. You study at home, alone.

When you complete an assignment, you mail it to the school. You do the same thing with tests. Your work is examined by your instructor. He or she grades it, writes down comments and suggestions, and returns it to you.

If your assignments are not well done, your teacher may suggest that you go over some of the material again, and give you advice on methods to use when you study. If you can't write well, you will be at a disadvantage. You may have to polish your writing skills before going on with the course. If you fail an examination, your teacher will point out where your weaknesses lie, give you assignments to help you overcome them, and give you another examination when you seem ready.

Most correspondence schools encourage their students to write or call (sometimes at a special toll-free number) whenever they have a question or a problem. Replies are prompt and to the point. The relationship between instructor and student is often as close as—or closer than—that between instructor and student in a regular classroom.

Correspondence courses have definite advantages over "in person" programs. They have distinct disadvantages as well. In fact, the advantages and disadvantages are opposite sides of the same coin. Think about them carefully before you decide that this kind of program is for you.

The good side: you set up your own schedule. You can study early in the morning, perhaps before you go off to a job; on your lunch hour; late at night or on weekends if that is what suits you best.

The bad side: it takes self-discipline of the highest order to stick to a study schedule that is entirely voluntary.

Correspondence courses are famous for the number of people who start them—and then just drop out without ever finishing.

The good side: because you work alone, you proceed at your own pace, which may be faster—or slower—than the pace you would follow if you had to keep up with a class of fifteen or twenty other students.

The bad side: you may miss the stimulation that being part of a class provides. Many students thrive on the give-and-take of ideas and encouragement that they get just from being together.

If you are highly motivated and well disciplined, you should do well in a home study program. If, in addition, you live where the regular schools do not offer the training you want, if you must work while you study, if for any reason you do not have the time or can't meet the schedule of an "in-person" program, a correspondence course may be just right for you.

What kinds of courses can you study at home? Schools offering correspondence programs can be divided into two major categories: private home study schools, and schools that are extensions of regular colleges and universities. The extensions offer the same academic courses that the colleges themselves offer. The private correspondence schools offer job training. At present, over 800 such schools exist, and over 2 million people enroll in them every year. Here is a sample of some of the vocational programs available through the mail:

Accounting
Blueprint Reading
Bricklaying
Business Writing
Camera Repair
Carpentry
Commercial Art
Computer Programming
Custodial Maintenance
Data Processing

Dressmaking
Electronics
Engineering Design
Engines and Engine Tune-up
Fashion Design
Flower Arrangement and Floristry
Guard Training
Heating and Ventilation
Housekeeping, Hotel and Motel
Insurance Adjusting
Jewelry Design and Retailing
Landscaping and Gardening
Locksmithing
Machine Shop Practices
Mapping and Surveying
Mechanics, Automotive
Piano Tuning and Repair
Plumbing
Shorthand
Tool Making and Design
Travel Agent Training
Typewriter Repair
Wildlife Management
Woodworking
Zookeeping, Beginning Levels

Most of the job training programs are carefully planned and thorough. They assume that the student is starting from scratch. For example, here is a close-up of the program in Interior Design offered by the International Correspondence Schools (ICS) of Scranton, Pennsylvania, one of the oldest and one of the best schools in operation. The program begins with the "first steps" of decorating and concludes with instructions for establishing one's own design studio or business. The course titles are:

The Art of the Interior Designer
First Steps in Decorating
Principles of Interior Design

[26]

Elements of Interior Design
Creating and Executing Successful Rooms
Practical Study of Period Furniture
The Professional Decorator at Work
Design Vocabulary

HOW LONG ARE THE PROGRAMS?

Since you are in a "class" by yourself, the length of time it takes to complete a program depends to a great extent on you. Most are designed to be completed in one to four years. But you can enroll for any time at all, and there is no "minimum" time limit. Even when outside limits are set, they can usually be extended. Almost every school, however, will drop you if you are "inactive" (if you send in no material, complete no assignments, take no exams) for over a year.

HOW MUCH DOES IT COST?

Individual correspondence courses cost anywhere from $100 to $1,000, depending on the nature of the equipment involved as well as on the nature of the course itself. Courses in the technologies may involve kits worth a great deal of money. They are, therefore, among the most expensive courses to take. In almost every case, however, the cost of a correspondence course is less than the cost of the same course in a regular program.

HOW TO APPLY

Before you even think about enrolling in a correspondence school, you must do some careful investigating. The field is full of fly-by-night operations that make the most wonderful promises, pressure you into enrolling, take your money, and give you nothing worthwhile in return.

You can't go wrong if the school in which you are interested has been accredited by the National Home Study Council, the recognized accrediting agency for correspondence schools according to the U.S. Office of Education.

[27]

For a list of the schools the council has accredited, write to the National Home Study Council, 1601 Eighteenth Street N.W., Washington, D.C. 20009. Ask for the *Directory of Accredited Private Home Study Schools.* You can also find the directory in the reference section of your local library.

Things would be simple if the council accredited all the good schools in the country. But it doesn't. It is up to the schools themselves to ask the council to investigate them, and many do not do so. In fact, of the 800 correspondence schools now in operation, only 200 are in the Council directory. For the names of reputable schools that have not been accredited by the council, call the office of your local Board of Education (check the phone book for a listing). The Better Business Bureau in your area and the State Employment Service (both listed in the phone book) are also good places to check. You can use the listings in the Yellow Pages of your phone book (under "Schools"), but keep your wits about you. Stay away from any school that:

1. Promises a glamorous, high-paying career after a few weeks of training.

2. Guarantees that you will be employed after you finish the program. (A good school will offer to help you find a job, but it will not guarantee one.)

3. Advertises "reduced fees for a limited time" or "limited enrollment." (These are methods used to pressure students into enrolling. Good schools do not use them.)

Zookeepers face challenges every day that don't often crop up in most jobs. While some on-the-job training is needed for this type of work, correspondence courses can provide basic information.

Finally, don't stop with the name of one school. Find as many as you can, and write to them all. Ask about: the methods used in grading lessons; the time it takes the average student to complete the program; the method of payment and the refund policy. Ask for: catalogs, course descriptions, sample lessons, and the names and addresses of students who are taking or have completed the course. Contact the students and ask them whether they are satisfied with the course they took and whether it helped them in the job market. There are many excellent correspondence schools offering excellent programs. But it's up to you to find them. Don't enroll in a school that does not answer your request for information, or in one that assures you that you will be pleased with the program but offers no hard facts about its contents.

For more information, write to the Council of Better Business Bureaus, Inc., 1150 Seventeenth Street N.W., Washington, D.C. 20036. Ask for its free brochure *Tips on Home Study Schools,* publication #229.

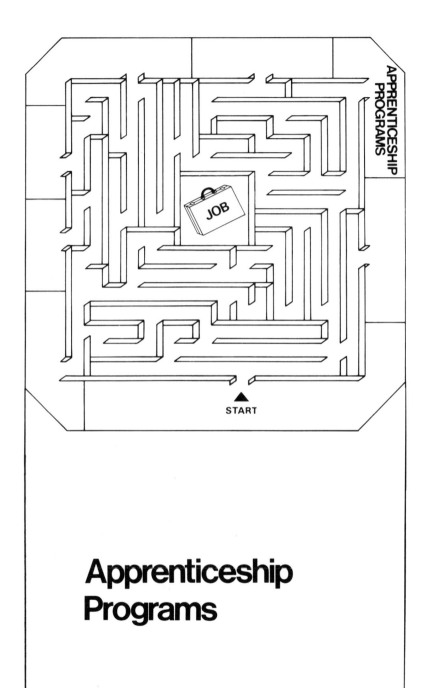

JOB

▲
START

Apprenticeship
Programs

WHAT THEY ARE,
WHAT THEY OFFER

The apprenticeship is one of the oldest methods of learning a skilled trade, and it is still one of the best. Apprentices learn a skill by doing it—under the guidance and instruction of an experienced or "master" craftsperson. When it is appropriate, apprentices are also given formal classroom instruction. They are paid a salary as they learn, usually about half the salary that a fully trained person receives. As they progress, the salary increases.

Many experts think that apprenticeship programs are the most efficient way there is to learn a trade. Though the heart of these programs is on-the-job training, it is quite different from the kind of training you might pick up on your own by working as an assistant to someone with experience. Apprentices are taken, step by step, through every aspect of the trade. They learn not just one skill but all the skills the trade involves. When they complete the program, they are "all-round" workers, able to understand the trade as a whole and to work in any branch of it.

Who offers apprenticeship programs? The "trainer" may be any employer who needs skilled workers. But most apprenticeship programs are developed and run by "joint committees" consisting of people who represent the employer and others who represent a labor union. The trainer and the apprentice sign a formal agreement that describes the program in detail: what the novice will be taught, and how; how much supervision will be provided, and by whom; what the novice's duties will be; what the starting salary is and when raises will be granted; how long the program will last.

The federal government supervises apprenticeship programs through the Bureau of Apprenticeship and Training, Department of Labor. Programs that meet the bureau's standards—designed principally to protect apprentices—are "registered." There are registered programs for over 400 different occupations today, from automobile mechanic to wood-carver. People who complete them are eligible for a

Certificate of Completion of Apprenticeship. With this certificate, they are recognized by business and industries throughout the United States as fully trained all-round workers.

Apprenticeships are offered only when and if there is a need for more skilled workers in a field. So all who complete an apprenticeship program are assured of excellent job opportunities. Their training also makes them top-flight candidates for promotion. In many industries, managers, superintendents, and supervisors are commonly selected from the ranks of those who have completed an apprenticeship program. A survey of companies in the construction industry found that 90 percent of the top company officials —presidents, vice-presidents, owners, and partners—began their careers as apprentices. If you want thorough training in a trade, virtually guaranteed employment, and real opportunity for advancement, an apprenticeship might be the thing for you.

HOW LONG ARE THE PROGRAMS?

Apprenticeship programs are lengthy. The exact amount of time varies with the nature of the work. Here is a list of some of the occupations for which registered apprenticeships are available, along with the number of years it takes to complete them.

OCCUPATION	LENGTH OF THE PROGRAM
Airplane mechanic	3–4 years
Baker	3 years
Barber	2 years
Bookbinder	2–4 years
Bricklayer	3 years
Butcher-meatcutter	3 years
Carpenter	4 years
Cosmetician	2 years

Draftsman-designer	3–5 years
Electrical worker	4–5 years
Farm equipment mechanic	3–4 years
Furrier	3–4 years
Glazier–glass worker	2–4 years
Jeweler	2–4 years
Lithographer	4–5 years
Musical instrument mechanic	3–4 years
Optical technician	4 years
Plasterer	3–4 years
Plumber–pipe-fitter	4–5 years
Roofer	2–3 years
Sheet metal worker	3–4 years
Stonemason	3 years
Tailor	4 years
Tile setter	3 years
Tool and die maker	4–5 years
Upholsterer	3–4 years
Wallpaper craftsperson	4–5 years
Wood-carver	3–5 years

HOW MUCH DOES IT COST?

An apprenticeship is a kind of job, and apprentices earn money while they learn. The starting salary is usually 40 to 50 percent of the salary of a fully trained worker. In most programs, pay raises are granted every six months. Salaries in the skilled trades—the trades for which apprenticeships

**Apprenticeship programs offer
the unique opportunity of learning
a trade under the instruction
of an experienced craftsperson.
The apprentice here is learning
to work with glass.**

exist—are very good. The average is $300 a week. So even half the regular salary would be enough to make ends meet. For example, you might become an apprentice in a trade that pays $7.00 an hour to fully trained people. You would start at $3.50 an hour. For the first segment of your training —say, the first six months—you would earn half the normal salary, $140 a week. In the last segment, you would earn 90 percent of the normal salary, about $250 a week. Throughout your training you would receive the same fringe benefits that regular employees receive, including health insurance and paid vacation time.

HOW TO APPLY

The local office of your State Employment Service is the place to get information about apprenticeship programs. You will find the number of the office nearest you in your telephone book. If you live in a large city or a major industrial area, the State Employment Service may operate a special Apprenticeship Information Center. Ask for it when you call. (These centers are set up by the federal Bureau of Apprenticeship and Training, but they are run by the state.)

If there is no Apprenticeship Training Center near you, the State Employment Service itself will help you. It should have information on all the programs in the state and in neighboring states. It will be able to tell you about the requirements of each program, the rates of pay—and most important of all, which programs are expected to have openings, and when. (Sometimes there is an opening immediately, but don't count on it. Lots of people want to get into these programs.) They will interview you and put your name on a list. When openings occur for which you seem eligible, they will give your name to the people in charge.

If you want more information than the State Employment Service can provide, look in your phone book under "U.S. Government—U.S. Department of Labor." See if there is a listing for the Regional Office of the U.S. Bureau of Apprenticeship and Training. Call the office, tell them the name of the trade in which you are interested, and ask about programs in your area. They will give you the names of local firms (if there are any) that have apprenticeship programs. Write to these firms and ask for detailed information.

If there is no listing for a regional office in your local phone book, write directly to the U.S. Bureau of Apprenticeship and Training, Employment and Training Administration, U.S. Department of Labor, Washington, D.C. 20210. Ask for the name and address of the nearest regional office.

Here are the basic requirements you must meet if you wish to become an apprentice. Individual programs may have additional requirements, depending on the nature of the work involved. Your counselor at the State Employment Service or the Apprenticeship Information Center can tell you what they are.

Basic Requirements

1. You must be between seventeen and twenty-six years of age (except veterans).
2. You must be physically and intellectually capable of performing the work involved.
3. You must be "morally fit" and have a letter of recommendation which states that you are.
4. It is preferred and sometimes required that you have a high school diploma or the equivalent.
5. You must agree to complete the program.
6. You must pass an entrance test.

If your background is weak, there are organizations that will help you prepare for the entrance test. First ask the people at the State Employment Service or the Apprenticeship Information Center. You should also call the local office of the AFL–CIO, the Urban League, or the Workers Defense League. Check your telephone book for local listings.

For more information, write to the Bureau of Apprenticeship and Training, Employment and Training Administration, U.S. Department of Labor, Washington, D.C. 20210. Ask for the booklet *National Apprenticeship Programs: Past and Present.* It describes the nature of apprenticeship programs and explains how they work. Also ask for *Jobs for Which Apprenticeships Are Available.* Both publications are free.

You should also write to the U.S. Superintendent of Documents, U.S. Government Printing Office, Washington, D.C. 20402. Ask for *Apprenticeship Training: Sure Way to a Skilled Craft.* This booklet costs 20¢.

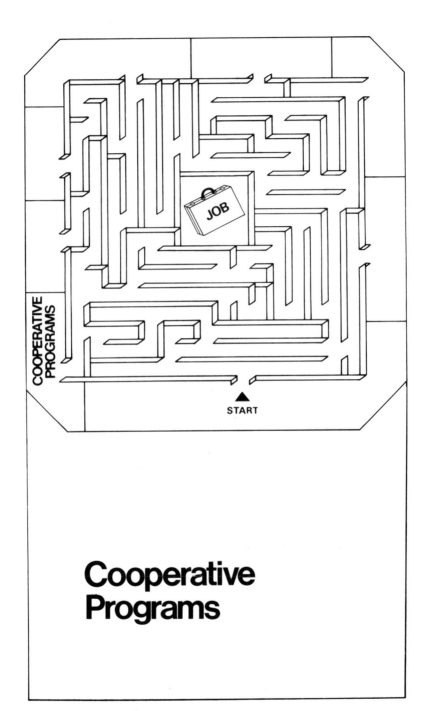

JOB

COOPERATIVE
PROGRAMS

START

Cooperative
Programs

WHAT THEY ARE,
WHAT THEY OFFER

Cooperative programs are programs in which the student attends classes for part of the time and works at a job for part of the time. The school itself oversees the student's schedule and arranges the job to be held.

Cooperative programs come in two varities: academic programs leading to a B.A. or B.S. degree, and vocational programs. The academic programs do not train students for jobs. Their aim is just to give students experience in the world of work, and encourage them to think in terms of employment, while they are still in school. Vocational programs are entirely career-oriented. Job and classroom complement one another and have a single aim: to develop the student's occupational skills and expertise. What you study in the classroom is what you use on the job in which the school places you. If you are studying bookkeeping, you will do bookkeeping on your job. If you are studying carpentry, you will do carpentry.

Students usually spend equal or almost equal amounts of time on the job and in the classroom, but the way the time is divided varies. In some schools, you would attend classes every morning and work every afternoon. In others, you would alternate by the week; in others, by the month.

Vocational work-study programs are offered at over 200 community colleges and technical institutes throughout the United States. Many educators think they are the best job-training programs going. Students learn, and they learn well. Graduates handle themselves and their on-the-job duties with ease and confidence. They know what the job requires of them and what it has to offer. They know what they are capable of doing, and what they wish to do.

The range of occupations for which work-study programs are available is quite broad. Most schools that offer them believe in them strongly and structure almost all their courses "cooperatively." The Carl Sandburg Community College in Illinois, for example, offers seventeen vocational

Cooperative programs allow students the chance to work part-time and attend classes on subjects related to his or her job part of the time. Fire protection is one of a long list of skills that can be learned this way.

work-study programs, from agricultural production to practical nursing and secretarial science. Bakersfield College in California offers twenty-five, including automotive mechanics, fashion merchandising, and journalism.

Here is a sample of occupational areas, along with the number of schools in the United States that offer cooperative programs in them.

FIELDS OF STUDY	NUMBER OF SCHOOLS OFFERING COOP-ERATIVE PROGRAMS
Accounting	60
Administration	25
Advertising	12
Aerospace Technology	20
Agriculture	55
Applied Mechanics	2
Architecture	40
Automotive Technology	40
Aviation Maintenance, Management, Control, and Administration	50
Building Construction Technology	16
Business and Business Administration	200
Cabinetmaking	5
Carpentry	2
Ceramics	4
Chemical Technology	9
Data Processing	70
Drafting and Drafting Technology	40
Electronics and Electronic Technology	50
Engineering Technology	14
Fashion Design and Fashion Merchandising	30

Fire Protection Engineering and Science	30
Food Distribution and Management Technology	35
Forestry and Forestry Technology	18
Graphic Design and Technology	10
Marketing	50
Medical Technology	45
Office Occupations	50
Real Estate	25
Recreation Technology	35
Retail Management	30
Secretarial Science	120
Teacher Aides	3
Welding	20

For a complete list of programs and the schools that offer them, consult the *Directory of Cooperative Education,* compiled by the Drexel Cooperative Education Association. You should find it in the reference section of your local library.

HOW LONG ARE THE PROGRAMS?

Most vocational work-study programs take two years to complete. A few, like the Practical Nursing and Secretarial Science programs at Carl Sandburg Community College, can be completed in one year.

HOW MUCH DOES IT COST?

If you attend a program in a community college, it may cost you nothing at all. In schools that charge tuition, the cost runs between $800 and $2,000 a year. The average cost is $1,200. The money you earn on the job, however, will decrease the total amount of money you actually spend for the program.

Students in cooperative programs are eligible for federal assistance. To find out about the programs, contact the Office of Financial Aid in the school in which you are interested, or write to Student Aid, U.S. Office of Education, Washington, D.C. 20202.

HOW TO APPLY

First, find the programs in which you are interested, and the schools that offer them, in the *Directory of Cooperative Education.* Write to the schools and ask for catalogs, course descriptions, and information about entrance requirements. Most schools require candidates to be high school graduates. Some will ask you to submit the results of an aptitude test, and some will want to interview you before they accept you as a student.

For more information about cooperative education programs, write directly to the Cooperative Education Association, Drexel University, Philadelphia, Pennsylvania 19104.

**Secretarial and clerical skills
can be learned in the classroom
and practiced on a job set up
through cooperative programs.**

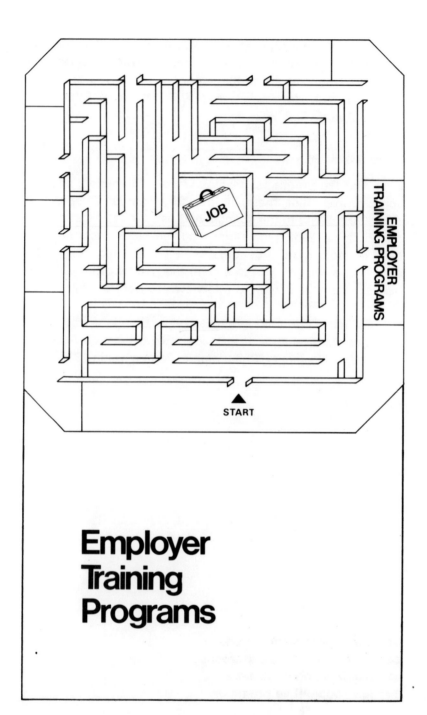

**Employer
Training
Programs**

WHAT THEY ARE,
WHAT THEY OFFER

In some industries, employers train their own employees. They hire young people straight out of high school and teach them the skills and techniques they need to do specific jobs. Companies in the technological industries— among them, giant corporations like IBM, Sperry Rand, and the Bell System—are far and away the leading employers in this regard. They offer a wide variety of programs for a wide variety of jobs. And they offer many opportunities for advancement. But other employers, like real estate brokers, insurance companies, automobile dealers, and hospitals, also hire inexperienced people and give them the training they need to do the job. And public service employers, like police and fire departments, have long trained their own. In all employer training programs, you receive a full salary while you learn.

IBM, for example, develops, makes, and services equipment so complicated and expensive that it has had to create its own training programs for the people who work on it. It hires high school graduates who have no skills and no experience but who seem capable and willing to learn. In its East Fishkill plant in upper New York State (just one of many similar facilities), high school graduates are taught to operate production machines—the machines that make computer components—in a training program that lasts about three weeks. But the in-house training does not have to stop at the production line. If you are good at your first job, IBM may assign you to more complicated work—and give you the additional instruction you need to do it. Though most IBM technicians—the people who build and maintain the equipment in its plants—have completed two years of training at an electronics school or institute, it is possible to rise from the ranks of the machine operators and become a "departmental technician." If you perform well on the job you have, if you are interested and seem to have potential, your supervisor may recommend you for IBM's own sixty-four week training course. If you pass the aptitude test, you will be given formal classroom instruction in electronics, math, physics, mechanics, and chemistry, as well as laboratory work and on-the-job supervision and instruction. When you complete the course, you will be qualified to assist the department manager in supervising the production line and dealing with whatever technical problems arise. In time, you may become a department manager yourself.

All IBM employees are encouraged to select from the many courses—fifty in the East Fishkill plant alone—that the company offers at no cost. They do not have to be related to the job you are doing. The courses—from blueprint reading to systems programming and mechanical drawing —may give you the skills and background you need to move to a different position in the future.

IBM also trains its own service representatives to repair and maintain its business machines, from electric typewriters to the newest teleprocessing equipment. Applicants are interviewed, given aptitude tests, and then placed in a six-week training program in a local branch office. There they learn to repair IBM's electric typewriters. After a few weeks "in the field," repairing typewriters in the presence of a regular service representative, they are eligible to take a seven-week course at an IBM training school. There, in classes of twenty students, they study the more complicated office machines, from adding machines to calculators and copying machines. Then they are returned to the branch office and assigned a territory of their own as "associate customer engineers." Of course, they are salaried employees throughout their training.

Hired right out of high school, many young people qualify for employee training programs. These young men are working on wire connections in a Bell Telephone central office.

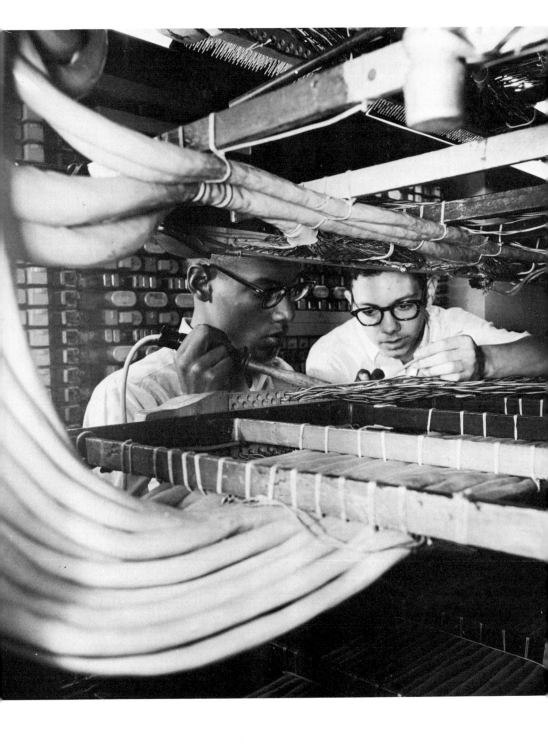

The Bell System—the giant electronic communications corporation—ranks right alongside, if not higher than, IBM as a company that trains its own. The Bell System hires thousands of high school graduates every year and trains them to manufacture, install, service, and operate its equipment. One entry-level job for which no skills are required is that of the lineman, who places telephone poles, cables, and wires out of doors. You would be trained for two weeks. Then you would join experienced workers on the job as part of a three-person crew. If you were interested and able, you you might receive further training and become an installer or repairer. You might go further and specialize—by means of formal courses conducted by the company—in teletypewriter or telephoto equipment, radio and TV transmission, or any one of a number of other kinds of special equipment the system manufactures. Or you might become a manager or a supervisor. Ninety-eight percent of the lower-level managers in the Bell System have risen from the ranks.

Telephone operators, too, are trained by the company itself in programs that take from two to three weeks. Operators have good opportunities for advancement. For example, all chief operators—executives who have total responsibility for the management of the office, and the training and supervision of new operators—are recruited from the ranks of the operators themselves.

If you are looking for solid training and almost unlimited opportunity, you won't find better places to start than IBM and the Bell System. None of the programs in either company is "for men (or women) only." Although there aren't nearly as many women as men in the technical and semi-technical occupations, and not nearly as many men as women in the telephone operating occupations, don't let that stop you. Both IBM and the Bell System are affirmative-action employers. They make every effort to consider every applicant on his or her own merits. If you are interested and think you have what it takes, apply.

Hospitals are another place to look for training programs, although they do not offer anything that compares in scale with what the technological corporations offer. Still, in order to be assured of the staff they need, they have begun to hire people who want to work in the health field but have no skills and no experience. High school graduates may be placed in training programs that prepare them to become ward clerks, ward secretaries, nursing aides, and orderlies. The programs usually take about three weeks to complete. Students in the clerking programs learn basic hospital procedures and record-keeping techniques. In the aide and orderly programs, they learn basic patient care, including how to bathe and feed the ill, and how to measure temperature, pulse, and respiration. For positions above the aide and orderly level, however, you must enroll in a formal course of study.

Many companies that hire sales personnel for house-by-house or person-by-person commission selling jobs train their employees before they send them out. (When you work "on commission," you get a certain amount of money from every sale you make.) High school graduates are hired and trained by automobile dealers, insurance companies, magazine distributors, encyclopedia companies, real estate brokers, and others. The training varies in length from a few days to a few weeks.

Fire departments, especially those in good-sized cities, almost always train their own staff members through classroom instruction and practice drills. The programs are usually one and a half to two months long. Police officers, too, are trained by the Police Department itself before they are assigned to duty. In small communities, recruits may learn by working with experienced officers. But in large cities, the training is formal and organized and may be anywhere from several weeks to several months long.

Most fire and police departments require applicants to be twenty-one years old. Check in your locality to find out what the age requirement is. Many police departments offer "cadet" or "trainee" programs for people who are not yet twenty-one. Strictly speaking, you would be a civilian and not a police officer. Your duties would be mostly clerical, but you would be able to attend classes in police skills and you would be considered a "preferred" candidate if, at the age of twenty-one, you applied for an appointment to the regular force.

For some jobs, all you need is quick and casual "on-the-job" training—the chance to work beside someone who has experience and can show you what to do. Waiting on tables in a coffee shop, over-the-counter selling, tending the pump in a gas station, and other jobs that do not require complicated special skills can be learned in a few days. Usually, new employees are considered "in training" for a week or two, however, which means that your employer will expect you to be a bit slow, to ask questions—and to make mistakes. After that you will be expected to have "learned" the job—to know how things work and what to do.

The job can continue to be a learning job if you are ambitious and determined to make it one. Fred Turner, for example, didn't know what to do when he dropped out of college. He took a job frying hamburgers in a local McDonald's. Today he is one of the company's chief executives, having "bubbled up through the ranks," as he puts it. There are other employers which, like the McDonald's Corporation, make a policy of promoting any employee who shows that he or she can do the job. But, in general, jobs that are very easy to learn do not offer much opportunity for advancement or change.

HOW LONG ARE THE PROGRAMS?

The length of time it takes to complete an employer training program depends entirely on the nature of the job the program serves. Some programs take one week, others two weeks, others several months to complete. More important is the fact that most employers who offer training programs for entry-level jobs offer additional training for employees who wish to advance. Bell System employees say that training "never" stops. The same can be said for IBM or any other large company that is technologically based. It is true in police work, too, though for different reasons, and in many selling jobs. In general, then, how long the training takes depends on how far you would like to go.

HOW TO APPLY

You can investigate local possibilities on your own. Check your telephone book for listings of IBM, the Bell System, or any other large-scale employer you might like to work for. If there is a separate listing for the Employment or Personnel Department, that is the number to call. Ask what—if any—training programs are available and what the requirements are.

Call and make an appointment to visit the local office of your State Employment Service. The office should have a list of all the employer training programs in your area. The staff will tell you what the requirements are and how to apply.

If you would like information about police work, write to the International Association of Chiefs of Police, 11 First-field Road, Gaithersburg, Maryland 20760. For information about fire fighters, write to the International Association of Fire Fighters, 1725 K Street N.W., Washington, D.C. 20006.

For a broad look at all sorts of programs and opportunities, check your local library for *On the Job Training and Where to Get it,* by Robert A. Liston. It describes a number of employer training programs—and a number of interesting jobs—in detail.

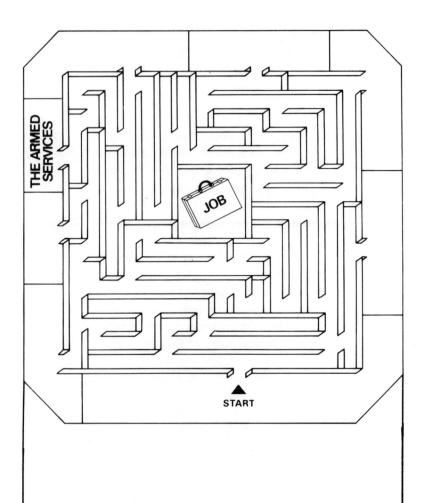

THE ARMED SERVICES

JOB

START

The Armed Services

WHAT THEY ARE,
WHAT THEY OFFER

The Armed Services—Army, Navy, Coast Guard, Air Force, and Marine Corps—offer so many kinds of career opportunities that it is easy to be enthusiastic about them. Being a member of the Armed Services can be a career in itself. Or it can be a stepping stone to a good career in civilian life. Every branch offers solid occupational training for jobs that exist both in and out of the service. Combined, the five branches maintain almost 300 technical and specialty training schools throughout the country, from which more than 300,000 students graduate every year. The programs are excellent. Some are among the best in the country. A few, particularly in the Air Force, can hardly be duplicated outside the service. All of them—except those for jobs directly related to combat—are open to women and men alike.

Programs are available in over 100 occupational areas, from Accounting and Aviation to Journalism and Topographic Engineering. You can learn to be an automobile mechanic, a cook, a career counselor, a keypunch operator, a photographer, a plumber, a weather forecaster, or a welder—to name a few of the jobs for which the Armed Services offer training. For a more complete list of job titles and a description of career opportunities in all the branches of the Armed Services, see *Careers in the Services,* by W. E. Butterworth (Franklin Watts).

Every branch of the Armed Services will guarantee to train you in the occupation of your choice—if there are openings in the program, and if you are qualified for it, as determined by aptitude tests the service gives you. The Army and the Coast Guard will test you before you enlist. If you are not qualified, by their standards, for the program you want, they will tell you so. At that point, you can decide whether or not you wish to join anyway. For details on Guaranteed Training Programs, call the Recruiting Center nearest you. You will find the listing in your telephone book under "U.S. Government—U.S. Armed Services." If more than one Recruiting Center is listed, call the number given

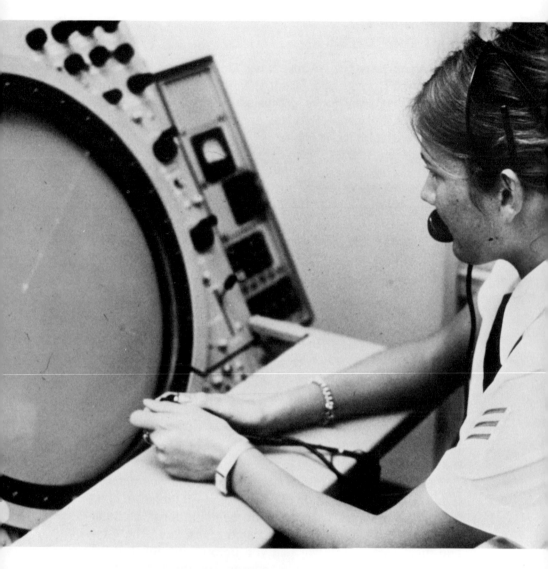

The armed services can prepare
you for several interesting and
challenging careers. Through
the Navy, this young woman
has acquired the position
of Air Traffic Controller.

for the Area Command. That office will have the most information and will be able to help you best.

The Armed Services also have programs for people who want to go to college, or to enroll in courses other than vocational courses. For example, while you are in the service, you can attend a college or university in your off-duty hours, and work toward a B.A. or other advanced degree—with the Tuition Assistance Program paying 75 percent of your tuition bill. If you are in the Army, and the curriculum meets an Army requirement, the government will pay the entire tuition bill and school-related fees, and give you money with which to purchase books as well.

There are many other kinds of programs and grants to help servicemen and servicewomen pay for higher education and training. For information about them all, speak to the Director at any Armed Services Information Center. Check your telephone book for the listing.

What is it like to be in the Armed Services? The first thing that faces all recruits is Basic Training. It varies in length from six weeks (Air Force) to eleven weeks (Marine Corps). You would "take" your training in a group of 55 to 100 others. Except for the Coast Guard, men and women recruits are trained separately. Normally, you would remain with the same group for the whole period. You would live together, eat together, and participate together in programs designed to build you up physically, including daily calisthenics, competitive sports, swimming, and foot marches. You would attend classes on service regulations, military insignia, military courtesy, rules of conduct, the handling and care of weapons (for men only), the Uniform Code of Military Justice, personal hygiene, food sanitation, and emergency first aid.

If you did not enlist under a Guaranteed Training Program, you would be given aptitude and classification tests and interviewed by a counselor during the period of basic training.

All this time, you would have to remain on the military base, but at certain scheduled times you would be allowed to receive visitors, attend movies, visit the library, and use the other facilities the base might have. From time to time, you might be given "liberty," or permission to leave the base.

At the end of basic training you would be assigned to duty or to a technical training school. After that, you would be assigned a specific military job. Most women in their first enlistment are assigned to posts and stations with a women's strength of fifty or more.

HOW LONG DOES IT TAKE?

Enlistment in the Armed Services is entirely voluntary. But when you enlist, you enlist for a specific period of time, and you may not leave before that time is up. Here are the enlistment periods for all the services.

Air Force: four or six years
Army: two, three, four, five, or six years
Coast Guard: four years
Marine Corps: two, three, or four years
Navy: three, four, five, or six years

The vocational training programs themselves may be as short as a few weeks or as long as several months.

HOW MUCH DOES IT COST?

You are paid a monthly salary from the moment you enlist to the moment you leave the service. Basic pay is determined by your rank or grade and the length of time you have been in the service. It starts at $361 a month. Of course, your military clothing is paid for, and so are your living quarters, food, medical and dental expenses, and any legal assistance you may need. You also get thirty days' paid vacation time each year, beginning the first year. Financially speaking, it would be hard to top what the Armed Services have to offer.

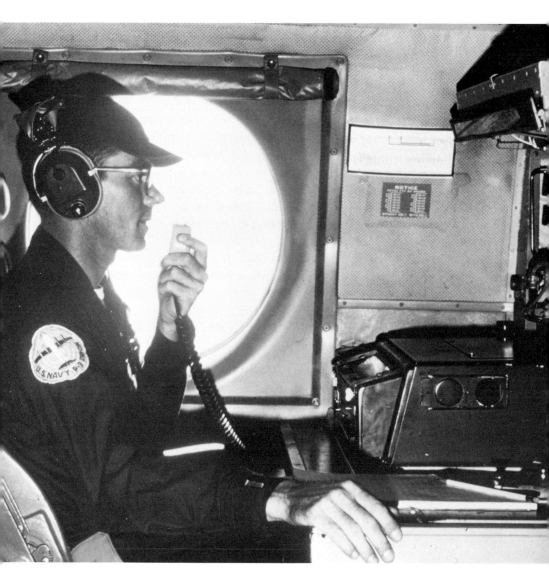

**You can learn about more
than ships in the Navy,
as this radiotelegraph
specialist will attest.**

HOW TO APPLY

The enlistment procedure for all the services is similar. Applicants must be interviewed, and they must pass tests to show that they are physically and mentally fit for military service. All the services, except the Coast Guard, will accept male and female applicants who are seventeen, if they have the consent of a parent or guardian. The Coast Guard requires women to be eighteen. All prefer applicants who have a high school diploma or the equivalent. But the Army, Navy, Coast Guard, and Marine Corps require it of women.

Your local Armed Services recruiter is listed in your telephone book. Call and make an appointment to visit and find out more about the different branches of the Armed Services and what each has to offer. Many training programs are available in all branches. But some are offered only by one or two. Ask for a copy of *Report: Basic Facts About Military Services,* and *VIEW: Vital Information for Education and Work.* They list and describe all the jobs for which you can be trained in the service.

Index